A Review of the 2001 Bonn Conference and Application to the Road Ahead in Afghanistan

A Review of the 2001 Bonn Conference and Application to the Road Ahead in Afghanistan

By Mark Fields and Ramsha Ahmed

Institute for National Strategic Studies
Strategic Perspectives, No. 8

Series Editors: C. Nicholas Rostow and Phillip C. Saunders

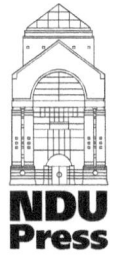

National Defense University Press
Washington, D.C.
November 2011

Opinions, conclusions, and recommendations expressed or implied within are solely those of the contributors and do not necessarily represent the views of the Defense Department or any other agency of the Federal Government. Cleared for public release; distribution unlimited.

Portions of this work may be quoted or reprinted without permission, provided that a standard source credit line is included. NDU Press would appreciate a courtesy copy of reprints or reviews.

First printing, November 2011

For current publications of the Institute for National Strategic Studies, please go to the National Defense University Web site at: www.ndu.edu/inss.

Contents

Acknowledgments

The authors are deeply grateful to Ambassador Lakhdar Brahimi, Ambassador James Dobbins, Colonel (Retired) Jack Gill, former Afghanistan Minister of the Interior Dr. Ali Jalali, Mr. Michael Kofman, Mr. Leo Michel, Ambassador Jeffrey Lunstead, Colonel (Retired) Thomas Lynch, Ms. Camille Majors, Dr. Paul Miller, Ambassador Thomas Pickering, Dr. Phillip Saunders, Ms. Sally Scudder, and Colonel (Retired) John Wood for either their detailed reading and assistance in editing this manuscript or their extended discussions of the substantive issues appearing herein.

Executive Summary

Ten years ago in Bonn, Germany, the United Nations Envoy to Afghanistan, Ambassador Lakhdar Brahimi, and U.S. Envoy to the Afghan Opposition, Ambassador James Dobbins, led a diverse group of international diplomats and warriors to consensus and charted the political course for Afghanistan well into the decade. The process that led to the Bonn Agreement (Bonn 2001, or Bonn I) reflects the best of U.S. and United Nations statesmanship and was the result of the effective application of military and diplomatic power. Bonn 2001 was successful for five reasons:

- The U.S.-supported Northern Alliance held the clear military advantage.

- The U.S. interagency position was effectively synchronized.

- Dobbins paved the way for success at Bonn by thorough bilateral preparation and consultations with international actors—he met personally with nearly all the international participants and representatives.

- Brahimi and Dobbins merged their negotiating experience and artfully used multilateral negotiations to meld national interests into cohesive commitments.

- Bonn Conference objectives were limited and achievable and the U.S. negotiating team was empowered to exercise initiative in pursuit of those objectives.

As the Bonn Conference's 10th anniversary approaches, the fundamental challenge is simply stated: how can U.S. national interests in Afghanistan be achieved with fewer resources? This paper answers that question through an analysis of the process that produced the Bonn

Agreement in 2001. It offers step-by-step recommendations for U.S. policymakers on how to shape specific conditions in Afghanistan, beginning with Bonn 2011 (Bonn II), for the post-2014 period. Those recommendations include:

- The United States must demonstrate long-term commitment to Afghanistan in the form of a formal strategic partnership announced at Bonn.

- Following Bonn, the United States must set conditions for a negotiated settlement through military and diplomatic means:

  - ▲ The United States should announce its intention to maintain a reduced military force in Afghanistan well beyond 2014.

  - ▲ The United States should fund the Afghanistan National Security Forces (ANSF) at the present manning objective (352,000) through 2015, then reassess this requirement.

  - ▲ The coalition should intensify efforts to kill or capture members of the insurgent leadership.

  - ▲ Bilateral preparation should begin with President Hamid Karzai and the issue of Afghan political reforms. Bonn I was about balancing control of central government offices. Following Bonn II, Afghans should rebalance power between the central government and provincial governments. Insurgents willing to lay down arms could play a legitimate role in local governance.

  - ▲ Bilateral preparation should then proceed to Afghanistan's neighbors and Russia, China, Turkey, and Saudi Arabia. This paper offers recommendations for dealing with each country in light of Bonn I and events to date.

Without U.S. commitment through the end of this decade, Afghanistan will likely fall back into the civil war it experienced in the early 1990s. As fighting spreads, India and Pakistan will back their Afghan proxies and the conflict will intensify. This situation would not only create opportunities for safe haven for extremists, but also invite a confrontation between adversarial and nuclear-armed states. The growing strength of Pakistan's own insurgency and the existential threat it could pose in the future intensifies this risk. The potential for such an outcome runs counter to U.S. and coalition interests. Bonn 2001 began a journey toward Afghanistan's stability and representative government that has demanded great sacrifice by Afghans, Americans, and other members of the coalition. That journey has come far from its humble beginning and requires American leadership and energy to remain on course.

Ten years ago at the Hotel Petersberg in Bonn, Germany, the United Nations (UN) Envoy to Afghanistan, Ambassador Lakhdar Brahimi, and the U.S. Envoy to the Afghan Opposition, Ambassador James Dobbins, led a diverse group of international diplomats and warriors to consensus and charted the political course for Afghanistan well into the decade. The process that led to the Bonn Agreement (Bonn 2001, or Bonn I) reflects the best of U.S. and UN statesmanship and was the result of the effective application of military and diplomatic power. Bonn 2001 began a journey toward Afghanistan's stability and representative government that has not been without its surprises and setbacks. It has demanded great sacrifice by Afghans, Americans, and other members of the coalition. But that journey has come far from its humble beginning and requires American leadership and energy to remain on course.

In December 2011, the international community will meet again in Bonn to consider plans for a stable Afghanistan. The successes and limitations of Bonn 2001 are worth remembering in preparing for that conference. This paper describes the process that produced the Bonn Agreement in 2001 and offers recommendations for U.S. policymakers on how to shape conditions in Afghanistan, beginning with Bonn 2011 (Bonn II), for the post-2014 period.

Bonn 2001: Why It Mattered

In December 2001, a diverse group of Afghans, influenced and supported by the international community, agreed to measures that established the foundation for future Afghan governance. Known as the Bonn Agreement, these measures established an interim authority for 6 months, under the leadership of Chairman Hamid Karzai, to govern Afghanistan until a transitional authority could be established by an emergency loya jirga.[1] The transitional authority would then govern Afghanistan for 2 years, convene another loya jirga to draft a new constitution, and hold free and fair elections. The agreement's authors also requested international assistance in the form of the deployment of a UN Security Council–sanctioned force to maintain security in Kabul "and other urban areas as deemed necessary," train Afghan security forces, and support general infrastructure repair and improvement efforts.[2]

Bonn 2001 was successful for five reasons:

- First, the U.S.-supported Northern Alliance held the clear military advantage. The Taliban were on the run by the time Bonn began.

- Second, the U.S. interagency position was effectively synchronized.

- Third, Dobbins paved the way for success at Bonn through thorough bilateral preparation and consultations with international actors—he met personally with nearly all the international participants and representatives. As a result, he understood the interests of the nations involved and how those interests could be productively leveraged.

- Fourth, during the conference, Brahimi and Dobbins merged their negotiating experience and artfully used multilateral negotiations to meld national interests into cohesive commitments.

- Finally, Bonn Conference objectives were limited and achievable and the U.S. negotiating team was empowered to exercise initiative in pursuit of those objectives.[3]

The Military Advantage

In late November 2001, the Northern Alliance dominated the Taliban on the battlefield. Such was not always the case. Understanding the Taliban's rise to power prior to 9/11 lends insight into the significance of the Bonn Agreement.

Following the Soviet withdrawal in February 1989 and the demise of the Soviet-installed government in 1992, Afghanistan was ruled by leaders of the mujahideen. A Tajik named Burhanuddin Rabbani became president in June 1992 and, at that time, agreed to step down at the end of 1994. In 1994, however, he refused to leave power. Elements of the mujahideen and Pashtuns in the south contested Rabbani's leadership. Pashtuns, who comprise about 40 percent of Afghanistan's population, felt that Rabbani was corrupt and anti-Pashtun.

In November 1994, after a year of organizing support among ethnic Pashtuns in southeastern Afghanistan, the Taliban peacefully took control of the southern city of Kandahar following the defections of key members of the local government leadership. In September 1995, the Taliban seized control of Herat and 1 year later took Kabul. Under the leadership of Mullah Mohammed Omar, the Taliban imposed strict Islamic rules. It prohibited women from working outside the house except for health care positions. It banned television and Western music and dance, and imposed harsh penalties—even execution—for those who violated these rules. Prior to 9/11, the Taliban controlled 75 percent of Afghanistan, including almost all of the provincial capitals.

The Taliban hosted and afforded protection to al Qaeda in Afghanistan. In April 1998, as U.S. concern over al Qaeda intensified, U.S. Ambassador to the UN Bill Richardson visited Afghanistan. Taliban leader Mullah Omar would not meet Richardson and refused to hand over Osama bin Laden.[4] In August 1998, al Qaeda operatives bombed U.S. Embassies in Kenya and Tanzania. In response, the United States launched cruise missiles at al Qaeda training camps in Afghanistan.

Following the 9/11 al Qaeda attacks on New York, Washington, and Pennsylvania, the George W. Bush administration decided to eliminate Taliban control of the Afghan government based on the extensive support the Taliban had rendered to al Qaeda and the U.S. need for open access to the country to eliminate its terrorist bases. On September 12, 2001, the UN Security Council passed resolution 1368 that "expressed [UN] readiness to take all necessary steps to respond [implying force] to the September 11 attacks."[5] On September 18, the U.S. Congress passed Joint Resolution 23, authorizing the President to use "all necessary and appropriate force against those nations, organizations, or persons he determines planned, authorized, committed, or aided the terrorist attacks that occurred on September 11, 2001, or harbored such organizations or persons."[6]

U.S. military operations in Afghanistan commenced on October 7, 2001, and focused on air strikes against the Taliban in support of the resistance forces of the Northern Alliance (Uzbek, Tajik, and Hazara tribesmen) and non-Taliban Pashtuns. Approximately 1,000 special operations forces and Central Intelligence Agency (CIA) operatives worked directly with the Northern Alliance on the ground.[7] In the south, non-Taliban Pashtuns led by Hamid Karzai along with 1,300 U.S. Marines fought to expel the Taliban from Kandahar. In November 2001, the Taliban lost Mazar-e-Sharif. On November 12, after unsuccessfully battling the well-fortified Taliban north of Kabul on the Shomali plains for 5 years, the Northern Alliance took Kabul. An estimated 2,000 Taliban were killed in 48 hours, most by U.S. airpower.[8] In December, when Taliban leader Mullah Omar vacated the city of Kandahar, the Taliban lost control of its birthplace in the south.

As events rapidly unfolded on the battlefield in favor of the Northern Alliance, Bonn Conference participants gathered at the Hotel Petersberg. The decisive nature of events on the ground encouraged the active participation of Afghan factions and international interests. The lightning fast shift in power significantly affected the interests of border nations (Pakistan, Iran, China, Uzbekistan, Tajikistan, and Turkmenistan) as well as Russia and India. The military advantage gained by the United States and its Afghan partners pushed the interested parties to seek a timely political solution rather than drawn-out and inconclusive peace talks. The various parties might have had different interests, but shared a concern that if an arrangement were not made, Afghanistan would repeat past tribal/civil wars and become the same hotbed of instability that gave birth to the Taliban and nurtured al Qaeda through the 1990s. This broad desire not to repeat the previous decade's mistakes brought a sense of urgency to the Bonn Conference and mandated a speedy resolution as the pace of the war accelerated. Each day the Northern Alliance held Kabul, Pashtuns saw a return to the unsatisfactory status quo of the early 1990s. Pakistan saw an existential threat given India's close ties and support to the Northern Alliance. Neither group would sit back and watch as events unfolded along this course.

Successful military operations also influenced the Bonn 2001 negotiating structure. Over time, four Afghan groups were loosely recognized by the international community as having a voice in the future of Afghanistan. These groups were the Northern Alliance; supporters of former King Mohammed Zahir Shah (known as the Rome Group because many had relocated there); former Afghan leaders in Pakistan (known as the Peshawar Group); and a group of opposition figures with links to Iran (the Cyprus Group).[9] Though the names and descriptions might signal otherwise, these groups did not each have a single position or, in some cases, even a pure ethnic makeup. Brahimi's initial vision of Bonn was an event exclusively limited to power-sharing negotiations among the Afghan groups in an environment free of outside influence.[10] Realistically, however, most of the Northern Alliance's recent battlefield success was the result of U.S. military power. It would be counterproductive to separate the United States from the negotiating process—U.S. "strong-arming" would be required to fashion a lasting agreement—especially when it came to power-sharing. The Northern Alliance would have to agree to cede much of its temporary power to the Pashtuns.

Dobbins, based on his negotiating experience in the Bosnia and Kosovo conflicts, recommended a different construct for negotiations—one made up of Afghans, the bordering nations, the United States, and Russia. Dobbins envisioned the potential for nations outside Afghanistan to apply pressure on the Afghans when needed in order to overcome obstacles and reach an agreement.[11] These situations did ultimately manifest and were solved using Dobbins's vision.

Effective military operations eliminated the Taliban's power in Afghanistan, brought diplomatic urgency to Bonn, and placed the United States in a position to leverage influence. How this leverage would be used in order to develop international consensus had to be sorted out first with the U.S. interagency, and then with the international community.

Shaping the Interagency Position

As the Northern Alliance made rapid military progress on the ground, the United States and UN needed to balance this progress with a diplomatic effort that established legitimate governance. The Bonn Agreement was born of this imperative. The achievement was the product of extensive efforts to set the conditions for diplomatic success that took place in the U.S. interagency and in the international community before the conference.

In October 2001, Under Secretary of State Marc Grossman assigned Dobbins as Secretary of State Colin Powell's Envoy to the Afghan Opposition. Dobbins had a 37-year career with State, which included key positions in Washington as well as experience as U.S. Ambassador to the European Community and negotiating experience in Somalia, Haiti, Bosnia, and Kosovo. Dobbins knew well the value of understanding and, where necessary, "refining" the interagency position before beginning negotiations. Directly following his assignment by Grossman, he met with the leadership of all the relevant U.S. agencies/departments in order to determine the U.S. position, identify agency "rice bowls," and chart out objectives and negotiating limits for the road ahead.

Though Powell issued general guidance—"We need to get this [a governance agreement/architecture in Afghanistan] done—speed, speed, speed"[12]—Dobbins quickly found that there was no single authority coordinating Afghan policy in the interagency below the cabinet level.[13] Despite the dynamic situation in Afghanistan, policy development and approval across the interagency could only be established among cabinet-level principals. No subcabinet-level officer could convene a meeting or task others to provide policy input or feedback. This practice, adopted by the Bush administration when it took office, reversed a practice established by the Clinton administration following the experience in Somalia, where a Presidential Decision Memorandum was issued directing the appointment of a single official, at State or the National Security Council (NSC), to oversee all policy aspects of any military intervention.[14] The lack of a similar process in the Bush administration was a problem for Dobbins, since cabinet principals were too busy to issue the type of specific guidance he needed before negotiating with the other concerned governments and Afghan factions. So he set about the task of determining—and in essence synchronizing and refining—the U.S. position on Afghanistan, acting on the basis of very general guidance and with a high degree of personal initiative.

Key contributors in Washington to the development of U.S.-Afghanistan policy were Zalmay Khalilzad and Frank Miller at the NSC and Christina Rocca (Assistant Secretary for South and Central Asian Affairs) and Richard N. Haass at State. Khalilzad, born in Afghanistan and educated there through high school, was the only Washington policymaker with first-hand knowledge of the country and its personalities.[15] Miller chaired an interagency working group that was almost exclusively focused on the military build-up in Afghanistan. Haass was the head of State's Afghanistan Policy Planning Staff and worked with Rocca. His job was to coordinate policy among four of State's organizations that managed policy for Afghanistan's bordering nations: the South Asian Bureau (Pakistan); the European Bureau (Turkmenistan, Uzbekistan, Tajikistan); the Middle Eastern Bureau (Iran); and the East Asian Bureau (China). From these meetings Dobbins pieced together a short-term U.S. position that gained consensus: the United States desired a broadly based, moderate Afghan regime that would reassure its neighbors and assist in stamping out residual terrorism.[16] In support of that objective and based on Afghanistan's history of resistance to foreign occupation and influence, the United States wanted to minimize foreign participation and influence in the future Afghanistan.

Dobbins also met with U.S. Ambassador to the UN John Negroponte. Together they discussed the UN's potential contribution and the Northern Alliance's reluctance to date to discuss power-sharing with other Afghan factions. Dobbins suggested a UN-sponsored conference to decide the future of Afghan governance—an idea developed by the Policy Planning Staff.[17] This meeting would gather all the factions as well as Afghanistan's neighbors and other countries with interest in a solution. Negroponte liked the idea and suggested the conference be announced at a UN-hosted meeting of Afghanistan's neighbors, plus the United States and Russia, the following week. Under UN sanction and leadership, the initiative could proceed with credibility.

In other meetings, U.S. Ambassador to Pakistan Wendy Chamberlain described President Pervez Musharraf's concerns that a Northern Alliance–run Afghanistan would align with Indian interests and threaten Pakistan. Pakistan had supported the Taliban in their rise to power, and Chamberlain emphasized Musharraf's post-9/11 announcement that Pakistan would cut support to the Taliban. Robert Blackwill, U.S. Ambassador to India, described the important support India had given to the Northern Alliance. Bill Burns, Assistant Secretary of State for Near Eastern Affairs, told Dobbins that Iran shared some U.S. interests in Afghanistan in that it opposed the Sunni-based philosophy of the Taliban. Iran desired the return of the two million Afghan civil war refugees who had settled inside its territory and also wanted to reduce the amount of Afghan opium that traveled through Iran on the way to the European market. In spite of the opportunity presented by shared interests, Burns also pointed out the fact that the administration had limited U.S. dialogue with Iran. All communication was supposed to be channeled through Swiss embassies in either capital. Dobbins was interested in exploring his ability to leverage mutual U.S.-Iranian interests in negotiations, but found that he would need Powell's permission to do so.[18]

At the Department of Defense, Dobbins met with Under Secretary Paul Wolfowitz and U.S. Central Command Commander General Tommy Franks. Dobbins surfaced with Wolfowitz the possibility that U.S. forces might be needed for a post-settlement peacekeeping mission. Franks reviewed operational details and emphasized the importance of maintaining a small U.S. military footprint.[19] Franks also indicated to Dobbins that Karzai had recently been safely extracted by the United States from the possibility of Taliban capture.

At CIA, Dobbins met with Deputy Director John E. McLaughlin and a group of experienced Afghanistan analysts and operators who discussed Afghanistan's recent history, the progress of ongoing operations, the role of specific warlords, and the role of the Pakistani ISI (Inter-Services Intelligence) in supporting the Taliban.[20] According to Dobbins, the CIA provided the very best insight into rapidly moving events on the ground and had positioned liaison officers with all the key warlords: Ismail Kahn in the west near Iran, General Abdul Rashid Dostum with the Uzbeks, Ustad Atta Mohammed with the Tajiks, and Qasim Mohammed Fahim in the northeast.[21] Resistance in the Pashtun-dominated south was far less organized or supported. The Taliban enjoyed greater support among its own tribe in the region and also from the Pakistani ISI. At CIA and the Department of Defense, Dobbins asked for and received a member of each organization to join his team; the representatives were to report developments and support requirements back to the home organization.[22]

Finally, prior to beginning his overseas mission, Dobbins met with the President's National Security Advisor, Condoleezza Rice, and her Deputy, Stephen J. Hadley. Dobbins briefed his mission to work with the UN and the Afghan resistance to quickly form a government. He recognized that the Northern Alliance could not unilaterally yield all the power. Afghanistan also needed Pashtun leaders not associated with the Taliban who had credibility within their tribe as well as with the ISI to share a powerful role in the government. Most importantly, he indicated he found general consensus regarding his mission and U.S. policy objectives within the interagency. Rice and Hadley were in agreement with Dobbins's plan and arranged for his transport overseas.[23]

By virtue of his previous experience, leadership ability, and willingness to consider the counsel of his professional associates, Dobbins anticipated many of the requirements he would later need to leverage an agreement at Bonn. In the absence of specific formal guidance and under significant pressure to launch his team overseas and demonstrate "progress," Dobbins took the time to meet personally with key interagency players. He not only became thoroughly informed on a region where he had no previous experience, he also informally established U.S. policy through personal contact and the exchange of ideas. He identified and engaged key decision- and policymakers within the bureaucracy—some who were layers deep and became key informal contributors. He anticipated and probed potential agency redlines that, if not identified early on, could have undermined his later efforts in the negotiations. By making personal contact and incorporating agency liaisons into his team, he built trust and confidence for his mission and personal credibility with the U.S. Government. He successfully introduced the idea of direct coordination with Iran—a concept that would prove indispensable later on as he and

Brahimi leveraged much needed international support at the 11th hour at Bonn. Finally, he transformed his informal coordination into official U.S. policy by receiving verbal approval for his plan from Rice.

Shaping International Support—Bilateral Preparation

During most of the 1990s, the United States did not have a coherent policy for Afghanistan or South Asia. In 1989, following the Soviet withdrawal, the United States closed its embassy in Kabul. Many in the government considered the U.S. mission in Afghanistan completed.[24] Beginning in 1997, however, under the banner of the United Nations, the "six plus two group" of nations (Afghanistan's six neighbors—Iran, China, Pakistan, Turkmenistan, Uzbekistan, and Tajikistan—plus the United States and Russia) began to meet to discuss the future of Afghanistan.[25] In 2000, another Afghanistan contact organization, the "Geneva Group," began meeting. This group consisted of Italy, Germany, Iran, and the United States. Though the work of these groups was criticized at the time as unproductive, they established a bridge for information and relationships that proved important in the post-9/11 environment. One of the most important contributions of the contact groups was knowledge of the nature and location of Afghan factions and former prominent political figures (Northern Alliance, Peshawar Group, Rome Group, and Cyprus Group). Brahimi attributes some of Bonn I's success to the coordination and working papers drafted by these groups under the leadership of Personal Representative of the UN Secretary-General for Afghanistan Francesc Vendrell.[26]

In October 2001, as the military situation began to change rapidly in Afghanistan, the UN named Brahimi to replace Vendrell, and in that capacity Brahimi was entrusted with overall authority for the UN's political, human rights, relief, recovery, and reconstruction activities in Afghanistan. Brahimi previously served as the Secretary-General's Special Envoy for Afghanistan from July 1997 until October 1999, when he resigned the position out of frustration at the lack of progress.[27]

At the UN, the idea for a UN-sanctioned conference on Afghan governance was taking shape. Brahimi led a group of representatives from the six plus two group through the wording of a joint statement calling for all Afghan opposition groups to meet under UN leadership to form a new government. He did not, however, want to announce the specific conference dates until he had a reasonable assurance that key participants among the Afghan factions would attend. Given the strength of U.S. contacts with and support to the Afghan resistance on the battlefield, Brahimi assigned Dobbins the task of obtaining that assurance.[28]

Dobbins used his assignment as an opportunity not only to coordinate Afghan participation but also to inquire into and, to some extent, align the positions of key nations. At the UN

General Assembly, Dobbins listened as the Iranian foreign minister—following a plane crash near LaGuardia Airport that was initially suspected to be a terrorist-related incident—said that Iran stood with the United States against acts of terror and expressed his sorrow for the loss of life. This Iranian gesture was significant given the icy relations between the United States and Iran, and opened the opportunity for Dobbins to engage the Iranians directly in negotiations on Afghanistan at Bonn.[29]

Dobbins began his mission to gain international consensus for the conference in mid-November. He met in Italy with King Zahir (age 87) and his supporters and secured their support. He then visited Ankara, since the Turks had good contact with Northern Alliance warlord General Dostum and had just hosted Pakistani President Musharraf. Turkish officials advised him to be sure to hold the conference in a nation that did not recognize the Taliban during their time in power. The Turks also suggested Karzai as an acceptable Pashtun resistance leader for the new Afghan government.[30]

Dobbins flew next to Pakistan, arriving on the same day that the Northern Alliance entered Kabul. In Islamabad, the Pakistanis made it clear that they would be hostile to any government headed by the Northern Alliance. As in Turkey, Dobbins heard the Pakistanis' suggestion—this time, from ISI director Lt. Gen. Ehsan ul-Haq—that Karzai should be named head of the Afghan government.[31] In Peshawar, Dobbins met with relocated Afghans who protested against the Northern Alliance's entry into Kabul. He also met with the governor of the Pakistani Frontier Province, who described the high degree of support that the Taliban had within his province and elsewhere in Pakistan. The governor also registered his skepticism about Pakistan's ability to follow through on Musharraf's commitment to cut ties with the Taliban.[32] In a separate meeting, Pakistani diplomat Rustam Shah Mohmand urged Dobbins to move with urgency as the situation in Afghanistan, in Mohmand's view, could quickly degenerate into the civil war experienced in the recent past.

Dobbins then stopped in Tashkent, where the CIA had persuaded Dr. Abdullah Abdullah, the senior Northern Alliance political representative, to meet him.[33] Abdullah argued that, despite U.S. reservations, the occupation of Kabul was needed to fill the vacuum left by the Taliban. He wanted the conference to be held in Kabul but noted he would consider other locations. In addition, he indicated that the Northern Alliance did not consider the Peshawar Group or the Cyprus Group of Afghans as negotiating equals to King Zahir's group. He also vehemently protested the recent entry of British soldiers into Bagram.[34] Dobbins downplayed the significance of the issues to Abdullah—decisions made at the conference would be based on consensus, not the size of the delegation. He also made it clear that the United States clearly understood the significance of the Northern Alliance contribution to events on the ground.[35]

Dobbins flew to Bagram, Afghanistan, with Abdullah where he met with the top Northern Alliance Commander General Mohammed Fahim. Fahim and Abdullah said that they were willing to "move forward to form a broad-based government which will represent all regions and all ethnicities."[36] Dobbins had secured what he came for—a Northern Alliance commitment on participation in the conference and a willingness to share power to form a government.

Soon thereafter, Dobbins and his team flew to Bonn to continue to set the conditions for successful negotiations just 48 hours ahead of the opening of the conference. He met with German diplomat Thomas Matussek who was assigned to manage activities at the Hotel Petersberg conference site. Though Brahimi wanted to keep the Afghan parties in relative seclusion, he understood the key contribution that Dobbins and his team would make. At Dobbins's request, Matussek gave members of Dobbins's team much needed access to the Afghan diplomats.[37]

Dobbins also met with other international representatives during the time before the conference began. Ambassador S.K. Lambha from India discussed his country's willingness to reach a governance agreement and promised to work closely with the Northern Alliance to get there. He also acknowledged the requirement for Pakistani support and did not pursue a hard anti-Pakistani line, despite the adversarial nature of Pakistani-Indian relations.[38]

Moscow sent career diplomat Zamir Kabulov who pledged his assistance. Like India, the Russians had supported and could influence the Northern Alliance. Kabulov also expressed his low expectations for the ability of the conference to produce an outcome. Based on Russia's very close ties with the Northern Alliance, he knew there were strongly divided opinions about power-sharing between leaders within the Alliance.[39]

On the evening before the conference, the Iranian delegation asked to meet Dobbins at their hotel. They indicated their position that former King Zahir was not a good candidate to assume the role of leader of the new government. They did, however, indicate that Karzai had their blessing.[40]

By the eve of the conference, within a month of assuming his duties as U.S. Envoy to the Afghan Opposition, Dobbins had made direct personal contact with the Indian, Russian, and Iranian delegations, the leadership of all four Afghan delegations, Pakistani key civilian and military leaders, as well as the Turks. He had not only secured the necessary commitments Brahimi had requested, he also found there was growing consensus regarding Karzai as Afghanistan's future interim authority chairman. These contacts and the knowledge gained would prove essential to his ability to overcome obstacles during the conference.

Brahimi, Dobbins, and Multilateral Negotiations

The Bonn Conference began on November 27. Following opening statements by the Afghan delegations, the conference settled into a routine series of parallel events.[41] At the Hotel Petersberg, Brahimi guided the main effort and focus of the conference: discussion among the four Afghan groups. As the conference was held during Ramadan, this discussion started late in the day and ended late into the night. Brahimi slowly worked to achieve consensus on draft documents that outlined measures for an interim Afghan government. Once delegates agreed to that design, he intended to work a power-sharing solution by gaining agreement on individuals for specific government posts.

Meanwhile, Dobbins, accompanied by his interagency team and Khalilzad from the NSC staff, coordinated the important but less visible effort of the international community representatives, who had access to the conference location but did not have access to Brahimi's formal meetings with the Afghans.[42] Dobbins assigned a member of his team to track the issues evolving in each Afghan delegation; he received a daily morning briefing from his staff regarding progress the previous night. Dobbins and Brahimi worked extremely closely together toward common objectives. They met daily to trade information regarding their negotiations or contacts and together developed plans to overcome obstacles.[43]

The Europeans, not fully aware that Dobbins had been empowered by Powell to talk directly to the Iranians, sponsored U.S.-Iranian contact sessions in order to facilitate coordination. When draft documents were distributed for review that described the governance architecture, it was the Iranians who suggested the document include the provision that Afghanistan hold democratic elections. The Iranians also suggested wording that indicated the new Afghan regime would be committed to combating terrorism.[44] Both recommendations ultimately appeared in the document.

As the agreement took shape, it mandated measures over time intended to establish an effective Afghan government. The Afghans agreed to establish a 6-month interim administration to govern the country. At the completion of that period, a loya jirga would select a transitional government that would govern for 18 months. This transitional government would draft a new constitution and establish elections for the new government to follow.

The Bonn Conference was initially scheduled to last 7 days. By the 10th day, Brahimi had achieved consensus on many of the structural issues associated with Afghan governance, but he lacked the essence of the power-sharing compromise—by-name recommendations for specific ministerial positions. One provision suggested by Dobbins was that the Rome Group, led by

King Zahir, be allowed to nominate the interim government's leader.[45] There was significant support and respect for King Zahir among Afghan delegations. It was common knowledge by most participants in the conference that Karzai was the only individual who could draw the consensus required among Afghans and the international community, specifically Pakistan, to fill this position. Despite these facts, the Rome Group wanted to nominate their own candidate, a scholar of Islamic Law named Professor Abdul Sattar Sirat. Brahimi, assisted by Matussek, quietly persuaded Sirat that he could not achieve the consensus required and he subsequently withdrew his name.[46]

Other issues associated with power-sharing, however, could not be solved exclusively among the Afghan factions and required leverage from the international delegations. Dobbins and Khalilzad had the ability to focus international influence on selected Afghan factions in order to gain consensus; for example, when the Northern Alliance entered Kabul, they filled all the key government postings in all the key ministries.[47] In order to achieve an agreement, they would now have to give some of those positions up.

Brahimi asked each Afghan faction to submit the names of their desired candidates for ministry positions. The Northern Alliance, on orders from Rabbani, stalled on the submission of these names for days. Younis Qanooni, the Northern Alliance's senior representative at Bonn, claimed that the Alliance could not achieve consensus from within and asked that the conference be adjourned so that the issue could be worked out later.[48]

Dobbins informed Deputy Secretary of State Richard Armitage and Powell in Washington, who in turn discussed the issue with the Russians. Dobbins and Khalilzad gathered the Indian, Iranian, Russian, and German delegates and outlined the critical nature of the problem, which could determine success or failure of the entire initiative. Khalilzad spoke directly to Alliance warlords Dostum and Fahim as well as Rabbani. Dobbins held a press conference to focus attention and pressure on Rabbani. On background, Dobbins told the press that Rabbani was "dragging his feet" in order to buy time in favor of the Northern Alliance.[49] The following day, after being informed that the Alliance would receive no more Russian support unless they accepted the "deal on the table," Qanooni submitted the cabinet nominations to Brahimi.[50]

The next day, the Northern Alliance raised yet another obstacle. They refused to give up the three key ministerial posts—defense, interior, and foreign affairs—and demanded 75 percent of the total cabinet positions.[51] Other Afghan groups would not agree. Again Brahimi, Dobbins, and Khalilzad asked the Iranian, Russian, German, and Indian representatives to meet with Qanooni and persuade him to compromise. After hours of fruitless discussion, the Iranian representative asked Qanooni to join him for a private discussion. In less than a minute, Qanooni returned to the group and agreed to give up two ministries and add three to the total.[52]

In the crucial final moments of the conference, working the most difficult issues, Dobbins, Khalilzad, and Brahimi maneuvered international interests to leverage concessions by the Northern Alliance and reached an agreement.

Limited and Achievable Objectives

In 2001, the U.S. strategic objective for Afghanistan was to establish a broad-based, stable Afghan government that, in the short term, would assist U.S. efforts to find and eliminate al Qaeda and, in the long term, would be stable enough to deny terrorists a haven. Supporting objectives included the military defeat of the Taliban, persuading the Northern Alliance to share power in a new government, gaining Afghan and Pakistani consensus on a new Pashtun leader, gaining the support of neighboring nations for a new Afghan government, and initiating humanitarian assistance with long-term "nation-building" (a term disliked by the Bush administration) and reconstruction efforts sponsored by the international community.[53]

Three of those objectives were assigned to Dobbins at Bonn: power-sharing, achieving consensus on a Pashtun leader, and gaining international support. These were limited, achievable, and well within the capacity of U.S. military and diplomatic power.

As previously discussed, decisive U.S. military power helped set conditions for success at Bonn. Support to the Northern Alliance gave urgency to the conference and enabled U.S. political influence with Alliance leadership.

The threat of military force also reduced Pakistan's ability to challenge or undermine the Bonn Agreement. Following 9/11, as the Taliban fled Afghanistan, Powell and Armitage delivered an ultimatum to Musharraf and the leadership of the ISI: "[Y]ou're either with us or against us."[54] Musharraf correctly interpreted the discussion as the direct threat of military force and decided he was "with us." He formally announced his intent to cut ties with the Taliban and support the United States. He subsequently opened Pakistani airspace to U.S. bombers and air bases to U.S. special operations forces.[55] In addition, Musharraf deployed forces to the border and arrested hundreds of al Qaeda fighters fleeing Afghanistan and turned them over to the United States.[56] At Bonn, Pakistan's interests were partially satisfied by the selection of Karzai, although Musharraf was not in position to demand more ministries be filled by Pashtuns given the situation on the ground and the ISI's recent support to the Taliban.

U.S. objectives at Bonn were also well within the capacity of—and were well served by—U.S. diplomatic power. The diplomatic team, working alongside the UN, identified and assessed the various national interests at play and focused their significant influence to overcome Bonn's highest negotiating hurdles. Diplomatic power—much of it in the form of Dobbins's experience and teamwork with Brahimi—produced a series of compromises that achieved consensus among the four Afghan negotiating groups. Gaining the support of neighboring nations, especially Iran, required a tailored approach but, again, one well within capacity.

In spite of significant U.S. policy differences with Iran, Powell loosened existing protocol (communication through Swiss embassies) and allowed Dobbins to interact directly with the Iranian delegation and to ask for and accept Iran's assistance in leveraging the Northern Alliance. Brahimi and Dobbins combined this leverage with pressure from Russia at precisely the right time in the negotiation in order to overcome the most difficult challenges associated with power-sharing.

Perhaps equally important was the limited nature of U.S. objectives at Bonn. Dobbins was not operating under a mandate to fashion a "U.S.-style democracy" for Afghanistan.[57] He was not required to fashion an agreement that ensured the long-term stability of the region—particularly with regard to Pakistan. President Musharraf had publicly reversed his country's position and committed his support to cutting ties with the Taliban, and Bonn's negotiations proceeded under the assumption that Pakistan would make good on that commitment. There was no requirement to fashion a role for the Taliban in the future of Afghanistan—they had been "defeated" and many at Bonn assumed the Taliban were down, out, and not coming back.[58] Dobbins's job was to minimize the U.S. footprint and structure an agreement that gave Afghans the opportunity to build a stable government over years. Given Afghanistan's history of fierce resistance to outside influence, it was understood at Bonn that "overreaching" might doom the project to failure.

The U.S. negotiating team was empowered to exercise initiative. Rice, Powell, and Armitage gave Dobbins and his team guidance regarding the endstate—get an agreement soon—and, with minimal restrictions, allowed him to freely coordinate and craft the solution with the interagency, UN, and international community.[59] Dobbins designed and built his team from among the interagency and used the best that each agency had to offer. He scheduled and adjusted his international preparation trip (Italy, Turkey, Pakistan, Uzbekistan, and Afghanistan) and interacted with international leaders without standard bureaucratic requirements, such as getting his talking points cleared by the interagency before each visit.[60] He negotiated from a variety of angles, held press conferences, and freely interacted on behalf of the United States as he deemed appropriate. Dobbins noted, "Things were moving fast, everyone [in the interagency] stayed in their lanes and we avoided elaborate [unproductive] discussion on what was going to happen next."[61] When Dobbins required assistance from his leadership in the form of transportation, access, or U.S. leverage, he received it.

As a result of limited objectives, effective multilateral negotiation, intense bilateral preparation, U.S. interagency synchronization, and decisive military action, leaders at Bonn produced an agreement that replaced the power vacuum and potential for civil war with fledgling Afghan governance. In spite of such significant achievements, however, much of Bonn's potential remains unfulfilled and, as a result, some have come to view Bonn critically.

Bonn—Critical Review

One common critique is that the Taliban should have been part of the negotiations at Bonn. According to this argument, if the Taliban's interests had been taken into account, the sacrifice and situation the United States and the coalition presently face would have been minimized or avoided.[62] Brahimi refers to the absence of the Taliban as Bonn's "original sin," but goes on to clarify that Bonn would not have been possible had the Taliban been at the table because of 9/11 and because other Afghan factions would not have allowed it.[63]

The critique regarding Taliban nonparticipation also discounts the reality of the time. The explicit U.S. objective was the expulsion of the Taliban from Afghanistan so that al Qaeda could be pursued and destroyed. More than an objective, this became a personal commitment from President Bush. Following 9/11, the American people would never have accepted direct negotiations with al Qaeda's sponsors in Afghanistan, since it would have been seen as rewarding an act of horrific terror with political concessions. The rapid progress of the Northern Alliance campaign, the decisive nature of U.S. airpower, the number of Taliban casualties, and Pakistan's commitment to assist U.S. efforts all led to the reasonable conclusion that the Taliban was on its last legs.

Another critique is Bonn's failure to address the problem of warlords. True, many warlords retained power years after Bonn adjourned.[64] But this critique ignores the reality of events on the ground. At the time of Bonn, the warlords who led the Northern Alliance to success on the battlefield controlled roughly 75 percent of Afghanistan. The expectation that the Bonn Agreement could somehow surgically remove warlords and their militias from Afghanistan's fundamental culture and power base was and remains unrealistic. Bonn had to be effective to avoid a civil war. The best anyone could reasonably expect was an agreement that structured transition, power-sharing, and compromise, which over time would evolve from a complete political vacuum to a relatively peaceful and stable government. A decade later that evolution continues to take place. Bonn's potential remains available.

Road Ahead

Much has changed in and around Afghanistan in 10 years. The government that was created from the Bonn Agreement struggles with corruption and incompetence in a security environment that U.S. leaders define as improving but "fragile and reversible." What has not changed, as reflected by Secretary of State Hillary Clinton's remarks below, is the U.S. interest and the fact that, just as on the first day of Bonn I, the problem of legitimate Afghan governance requires a political solution:

> *After he took office, President Obama launched a thorough review of our policy and set out a clear goal: to disrupt, dismantle, and defeat al-Qaida, and prevent it from threatening America and our allies in the future. Al-Qaida cannot be allowed to maintain its safe haven, protected by the Taliban, and to continue plotting attacks while destabilizing nations that have known far too much war. From the Tigris to the Indus, the region will never live up to its full potential until it is free of al-Qaida and its creed of violence and hatred. That is an aspiration that should unite every nation. In pursuit of this goal, we are following a strategy with three mutually reinforcing tracks—three surges, if you will: a military offensive against al-Qaida terrorists and Taliban insurgents; a civilian campaign to bolster the governments, economies, and civil societies of Afghanistan and Pakistan to undercut the pull of the insurgency; and an intensified diplomatic push to bring the Afghan conflict to an end and chart a new and more secure future for the region.*[65]

As the 10th anniversary conference approaches and in the context of the formal date of full transition to Afghan control in 2014, the fundamental challenge is simply stated: how can the United States achieve the objectives outlined in Secretary Clinton's remarks with fewer resources? The realities of waning U.S. and coalition domestic support for the war and its heavy financial demands, announced U.S. and coalition troop reductions, and anticipated reductions in funding for the Afghan army and police are certainly not a portent of the success that characterized Bonn I. Bonn II, therefore, must emulate Bonn I by achieving modest objectives and setting conditions for the implementation of additional measures through the transition in 2014 and the balance of the decade.

The United States must clearly demonstrate long-term commitment to Afghanistan in the form of military action and support, assistance with governance and rule of law programs, and economic development through this decade. This commitment should take the form of a formal strategic partnership endorsed by both nations and announced at Bonn II. It should reflect planned troop reductions of 10,000 this year and a total of 33,000 by the end of summer 2012, but maintain U.S. advisory and counterterrorism capabilities beyond 2014. It should also reflect sustained U.S. assistance through a reassessment period in 2015 that prioritizes rule of law and good governance initiatives (per the 2012 budget request for $5.25 billion in non–Afghan National Security Forces funding in the form of Economic Support Funds, Commander's Emergency Response Program funds, and other programs).[66] Bonn II should frame Afghanistan as a work in progress, but one that has made gains in security and governance since 2001 and one that will continue to experience progress with U.S. assistance and regional leadership and the support of the coalition. Demonstrating U.S. and coalition commitment should be the exclusive objective for Bonn II.

Following Bonn II, the United States must continue to assist Afghanistan consistent with the strategic partnership. In addition, ideally by 2015, it must set conditions for a negotiated settlement with insurgents through military and diplomatic means. One essential condition applies to internal Afghan governance reforms. A strong central government was required at the time of Bonn I, given the country's history of factions, warlords, and militias as well as the urgency of the situation on the ground. Bonn I was about balancing control of central government offices (president, vice presidents, and ministers) among ethnic minorities. Following Bonn II, however, Afghans should begin the work of rebalancing power between the central government and the provincial governments. This change will produce more responsive local government, allow for better political representation of Afghanistan's ethnic minorities, and increase the potential for a negotiated settlement by appealing to Afghans (including the Taliban) and international actors (including Pakistan). Ultimately, once conditions are set, the United States must use its power to leverage international influence to produce a negotiated settlement.

Though the conditions surrounding Bonn I differ from today, the factors associated with Bonn's success (military advantage, limited and achievable objectives, thorough bilateral preparation, skilled multilateral negotiation, and U.S. interagency synchronization) lend insight to the recommendations for the road ahead offered above.

Military Advantage?

Ten years of fighting and the lack of decisive progress have replaced post-9/11 U.S. and international consensus and commitment with skepticism toward a positive outcome in Afghanistan. The coalition does not possess the overwhelming military advantage it held in 2001/2002. The Taliban is not on the run as it was a decade ago.

The Taliban has experienced, however, a number of tactical defeats in its birthplace in and around Kandahar. A large number of middle and upper-level Taliban leaders, as well as insurgent leaders in the east, are being killed and captured as a result of a tremendously successful intelligence and operational effort by coalition special operating forces. These successes have been defined by the coalition leadership as "fragile and reversible" and require sustained follow-up by the Afghan army and police as well as governance/development measures.

Further magnifying the challenge are the announced complete transition to Afghan-controlled security in 2014 and the drawdown of coalition forces that will take place between now and then. The announcement of this date—and lack of clarity by the coalition regarding its willingness to keep troops in Afghanistan after 2014—has encouraged insurgents to "wait it out" in anticipation of the day when they will exclusively fight against the Afghan National Army. In addition, insurgents receive sanctuary in Pakistan and support from the ISI. The Pakistani government is challenged by its own insurgency and does not demonstrate the capacity or will to deny this sanctuary or support.

Acknowledging the lack of a clear military advantage, the military instrument of power must be further applied to create the momentum required to influence a political solution in three ways.

- First, the United States should announce its intention to maintain a military force in Afghanistan well beyond 2014, at least through the next Afghan political administration in 2019. This force would sustain the tempo of counterterrorist operations and provide professional advice and enablers to the Afghan army and police. It should number 10,000 to 25,000 personnel and could be reduced as the ANSF demonstrate their post-transition competence through the 2014 elections and into the next political administration. It could also be reduced by coalition contributions. Counterterror operations (supported by 3,000 to 5,000 coalition special operating forces) should focus on al Qaeda's attempts to relocate in remote areas of Afghanistan as well as target the leadership of insurgent groups who refuse to reconcile and continue to challenge the stability of the government. Advisory and enabling forces (supported by two brigades and supporting aviation) should focus on the professional development and training of the Afghan army and police as well as their effective performance in the field.

- Second, the United States and NATO should continue to provide funds to resource the ANSF at its present manning objective (352,000) through 2015, then reassess this requirement—including both the size of Afghan security forces and associated funding—based on security conditions. Funding for the period through 2015 should be consistent with but not fall below recently announced reductions from $12.8 billion to just under $6 billion per year.[67]

- Finally, without public announcement, the coalition should intensify efforts to kill or capture members of the insurgent leadership, especially Mullah Omar and his deputies. This will not only require a sustained and enhanced investment of intelligence, reconnaissance, and surveillance assets, but will also require intensified leverage on the government of Pakistan and the ISI. Omar's ideological commitment to extremist philosophy during his sustained term as "leader of the faithful" enhances his value as a target. Some believe Omar has the potential to represent the Taliban in negotiations. However, his demands for the immediate departure of all foreign troops from Afghanistan and his extension of sanctuary to al Qaeda make him an unlikely candidate for such a role. His capture or death would intensify the growing divide between the Taliban's working class fighting the war in Afghanistan and their leadership living in the safety of Pakistan.

These military efforts set conditions for political progress in four ways. First, they demonstrate to the insurgents that pursuit of a military solution will continue to extract a very heavy toll and, though they may be able to gain the upper hand at times in selected areas, they have no chance of reversing the security situation throughout the country as they did in the early 1990s. Second, these efforts will continue to provide time for Afghan political reforms to take effect. Many are already beginning to take shape. Third, they will continue to separate hard-core ideological insurgents from those more willing to reconcile, reintegrate, and pursue solutions through political means. Fourth, they will signal to nearby and neighboring nations—Pakistan, Iran, and India—that they will not be able to fill the vacuum created by coalition departure and the resulting instability in pursuit of their own interests at Afghanistan's expense.

Limited Objectives—Bonn II

U.S. objectives for Bonn II, for the period between Bonn II and 2014, and for post-2014 Afghanistan must be set consistent with our ability to accomplish them through diplomatic and military power. As stated, the coalition lacks the decisive military advantage and the international consensus it had in 2001. International momentum for governance and military initiatives in Afghanistan has been replaced, in the United States as well as in Europe, by fatigue and domestic political pressure for withdrawal.

U.S. objectives for Bonn II should be modest and focus on demonstrating long-term commitment to Afghanistan's security and development through the decade. The United States should announce a formal long-term strategic partnership with Afghanistan that includes the military support described above, continued assistance with governance and law and order reforms, and sustained development efforts. Following this demonstration of leadership, the United States should also begin work at Bonn to quietly secure similar long-term commitments of troop and development resources from coalition members. Bonn II should also highlight the progress to date of security efforts in the south, the development of the ANSF, the fact that transition is on schedule, the work of the High Peace Council on reintegration and reconciliation, and the evolution of women's rights since 2001. Bonn II should in no way create or fuel expectations of an immediate negotiated peace settlement in Afghanistan nor should it be the forum to address any changes in regional strategy.

Objectives Following Bonn II to 2014 and Beyond

Once U.S. commitment to Afghanistan is formalized at Bonn, the conditions for a final settlement can be addressed, following the model set by Dobbins and Brahimi, thorough bilateral preparation and multilateral negotiation. Bilateral preparation should begin first and foremost with the Afghan government—President Karzai—and the issue of Afghan political reforms. Bilateral preparation should then proceed to neighboring nations. Coalition initiatives (for example, troop contributions and economic assistance) should be announced consistent with the desires of the Afghan leadership.

Bilateral Preparation for Negotiations

As in Bonn I, comprehensive bilateral preparation must precede the negotiation of a political settlement with the insurgents. That preparation must begin between the United States and President Karzai—negotiations cannot be successful without a consolidated position between the two. President Karzai's recent surprise announcement, shifting the direction of primary peace negotiations from engagement with insurgents to engagement with the government of Pakistan, is the most recent example of the divide: "The peace process which we began is dead," stated Afghan National Security Advisor Rangin Dadfar Spanta.[68] Brahimi is very critical of the fact that Americans and Afghans have been fighting together for 10 years and have not worked out clear consensus on a political solution.[69] He observes that both countries must agree on a framework for a political solution before any other actors are brought in. Only after that consensus is achieved can the division of labor—discussions regarding positive international roles in the solution—be decided. Brahimi sees the opposite going on: "everyone is being given a piece of the labor before you and the Afghans have defined a solution."[70]

Once trust is reinforced through a U.S. long-term commitment to Afghanistan, President Karzai should be encouraged to improve governance by empowering provincial governments and reducing corruption. Both measures are essential to the condition-setting that must take place prior to negotiations with insurgents. The United States should seek President Karzai's commitment to implement governance reforms that empower the Afghan provinces, even if these reforms do not take full effect before Karzai leaves office in 2014. President Karzai may be persuaded to consider reforms in exchange for the long-term assistance offered in the strategic partnership. Other forms of persuasion may be rewards or penalties associated with the Kabul Bank crisis, the suspension of the International Monetary Fund's (IMF's) program in Afghanistan, and a potential large-scale IMF audit.[71] Each province must be granted the right to select its own governor and to employ independent fiscal, legislative, and conflict resolution powers. Provincial government employees should be hired from within the province and answer to provincial leaders. International financial aid should be funneled directly to the provinces in order to create rapid public support. These measures, over time, would bring the power and resources of the government to parts of the country where Kabul's leadership is viewed as corrupt and incompetent. At the same time, anti-corruption efforts from within the government must be intensified. Continued coalition and international assistance through this decade in the form of advice, investigation, and prosecution is essential. More effective local governance and courts would also serve to undermine the appeal of local conflict resolution currently offered by insurgents.

Many of these recommendations have already been planned, documented, and initiated. The Afghan government has published a thorough subnational governance policy.[72] This policy is comprehensive and, if resourced, supported, and given time, would significantly enhance the contribution of local government to Afghan quality of life. This will take time and require the continued commitment of the United States and the coalition to educate Afghan civil servants. This policy appropriately calls for and schedules elections of provincial, district, and village councils and should be modified to incorporate the election of provincial and district governors. In order to implement changes that empower subnational governance, the constitution will have to be modified. In order to effect those changes, a constitutional loya jirga should be assembled following the 2014 national elections to establish measures that allow the election of provincial governors. It is important that this measure follow presidential elections so that provincial councils can mature and so that the loya jirga would not be used to extend the term of the present Afghan administration. The initiative should be a part of Afghanistan's national dialogue in the run-up to the election.

Afghans should also consider the creation and installation of a prime minister. Presently, broad powers are assigned to the president by the constitution: appointment of cabinet ministers, members of the Supreme Court, provincial governors, district governors, and local security chiefs.[73] These powers are too broad for execution by a single individual, lack credible checks and balances, and invite the perception and reality of corruption. This change would also have to be considered by the loya jirga.

Following alignment of the U.S.-Afghan political position, bilateral preparation to achieve a negotiated settlement should, in many ways, follow the model of Bonn I. The United States should work directly with and urge the UN to sponsor the initiative by first identifying a credible UN Envoy, equal in reputation and diplomatic skill to Brahimi, to lead negotiations. The present Special Representative of the UN Secretary-General to Afghanistan, Staffan de Mistura, may be precisely the right individual for this position. However, the job of lead negotiator requires an exclusive focus. Together, the United States and UN must then identify credible Afghans who represent elements of the insurgency (Quetta Shura Taliban, Hikmatyar Faction, and the Haqqani Faction). In addition, negotiators for the Afghan government must include Pashtuns as well as Northern Alliance representatives. Just as at Bonn, the Northern Alliance will be particularly sensitive to the possibility that they will be required to give up power in the form of ministerial assignments. As evidenced by the recent assassination of former Afghan President Rabbani, the process of identifying who can speak credibly for selected insurgent factions—a job that requires personal courage as well as popular consensus—may take months. In the shadow of Rabbani's death, achieving the trust required for negotiations will be harder to come by. It is very likely that hard-core ideologues will have no interest in discussions—in which case talks should proceed without them and include as much moderate insurgent representation as possible.

Once credible representatives are identified, the UN should announce its initiative publicly. A schedule of discreet meetings should be set between now and the end of 2012. These meetings should evolve from discussions among mid-level representatives who exchange views on details and negotiating positions to meetings among deputies and finally direct representatives empowered to speak for their respective leadership.

The United States should take the lead in bilateral preparation of the six plus two group— and, in addition, include Turkey and Saudi Arabia. As the moral center of Sunni Islam and as financial sponsors of many of the Wahabis in Pakistan who fuel the insurgency's ranks, Saudis may be persuaded to provide additional leverage on elements of the Taliban to negotiate rather than continue fighting. Turkey, based on historic relationships, could offer a moderate Taliban element—one serious about negotiations—an office in their country and open an exchange of ideas and moderate discussion.

In spite of more recent diplomatic obstacles, the United States should work closely with Iran in this endeavor and build on Iranian interest in limiting Taliban-sponsored drug trafficking into their country as well as Iran's historic ties to the Northern Alliance. Russia, Turkmenistan, Uzbekistan, and Tajikistan also have an interest in curtailing the flow of drugs into their countries and, like Iran, an interest in stability across Afghanistan's northern border, and can leverage historic ties with the Northern Alliance.[74]

Pakistan's assistance in a long-term settlement is essential and will be the most difficult obstacle in this process. Obtaining its full commitment to eliminate sanctuary and support for Afghan insurgents while preserving a relationship in our interests is beyond the capability of U.S. power—the last 10 years have clearly demonstrated that fact. The skepticism regarding the government of Pakistan's willingness to cut ties with the Taliban expressed by then North-West Frontier Province Governor Shah to Dobbins 10 years ago in Peshawar was accurate and remains unchanged.

Expectations should be set accordingly. In the short term, it will be important to seek a Pakistani commitment to limit active support to insurgent groups interested in undermining peace initiatives. The United States should consider leveraging the significant amount of U.S. foreign aid funneled into Pakistan against this objective, as well as offering the Pakistanis a major role in the negotiation process. Specific arrangements, consistent with the concept of the empowerment of provincial governments, extending more autonomous political power within the provisions of the Afghan constitution to factions in Afghanistan's eastern and southern provinces, could be considered. The United States should also explore teaming with the Chinese to influence the outcome as they may possess an increasing amount of leverage on the Pakistanis.

Multilateral Negotiation

Following thorough U.S.-led bilateral preparation, and the identification of initial negotiating positions, the UN should host a series of multilateral conferences—similar to Bonn in that the UN Envoy facilitates negotiations between Afghans and insurgent factions and the United States facilitates and leverages international actors and power in the pursuit of a settlement. These conferences should begin prior to Afghanistan's 2014 elections—with the pre-election goal of a commitment to an announced ceasefire. Talks should progress through the election and the constitutional loya jirga and, ideally, announce a settlement soon after the loya jirga.

Synchronizing the Interagency

Synchronizing the interagency should not require the degree of personal initiative displayed by Dobbins 10 years ago. With regard to Afghanistan, the process has been institutionalized. The Special Representative for Afghanistan and Pakistan office, under the leadership of Ambassador Marc Grossman, has been the government's lead for consolidating interagency input and developing U.S. policy recommendations for the routine cycle of Deputies, Principals, and NSC meetings. This process, however, should not replace the requirement for personal contact by leaders within the interagency—face-to-face meetings that engender trust, confidence, and support for the U.S. negotiating position and negotiators—just as Dobbins experienced. The fact that this process will be significantly longer and more difficult to achieve than the Bonn Agreement further magnifies the importance of continuous interagency synchronization and support for the negotiating team.

Critical Views

The recommendations described above offer a plan to achieve success in spite of diminished U.S. and coalition resources over the next 2-plus years. This raises the question of whether a successful solution can be achieved with fewer resources given the fact that success has eluded the resource-intensive approach followed to date. The key to achieving success lies in the momentum previously established through the training, fielding, and employment of the Afghan army and police, intensified targeting of insurgent leadership by special operations forces, and the credible offer of a legitimate political role for members of the Taliban who wish to come in. The Afghan army is moving toward independent capability and its demonstrated performance in the field has steadily improved, most recently in the Taliban's birthplace in and around Kandahar. Intensified efforts at professionalizing the Afghan police began only 4 years ago, well after the army effort began, and their size and proficiency, especially in the Afghan Civil Order Police, are steadily improving. These improvements would continue under the proposed advisory force. Maintaining a counterterrorist force in Afghanistan that captures or kills insurgent leaders would continue to drive the wedge that has already developed between insurgents in the field and their leadership in Pakistan. Most importantly, political reforms empowering the provinces would undercut insurgent support by improving local governance while also providing insurgents the ability to address legitimate political concerns through participation in local and national governance.

A second critical view of the recommendations applies to corruption. Will rebalancing power between the central and provincial governments reduce corruption or simply transfer it to a lower level? The reforms suggested call for the election of district and provincial governors and the distribution of resources to them. Elections install a measure of local accountability not previously applied in Afghanistan and make government officials more responsive to their constituents. Provinces that spend money responsibly and effectively could be rewarded with additional government and assistance funds. Elections also offer new options to citizens unhappy with the performance of the level of government that, in Afghanistan, most influences daily life. Local governance would operate more along ethnic lines where the time-honored Afghan institutions of elders and shuras reinforce fair conflict resolution and equitable behavior.

A final concern is whether the U.S. Government can garner the necessary domestic and international support to extend the effort in Afghanistan through the decade. The answer lies in a realistic analysis of the U.S. national interest. Left on its own as U.S. assistance and influence declines, Afghanistan will very likely fall back into the civil war it experienced in the early 1990s between the tribes of the Northern Alliance and the Pashtuns. Other actors will move quickly to leverage their own security and ideological interests. Consistent with history and present alliances, India will back its proxies in the north and Pakistan will back its proxies in the east and south. The situation would not only create opportunities for safe haven for extremists, but would also invite a confrontation between adversarial, nuclear-armed states. The growing strength of Pakistan's own insurgency and the existential threat it could pose in the future intensify this risk. In addition, Saudi-funded conservative Wahabi groups will attempt to expand the spread of radical Islamic rhetoric to future generations of Afghan children who, as a result of declining assistance, will have no other options. These facts have precedent in recent history and their potential clearly runs counter to U.S. and coalition interests.

Conclusion

Afghanistan remains critical to U.S. interests. Despite the country's long history of tribal conflict, civil war, and foreign occupation, the rest of this decade will bridge the difference between unfulfilled potential and a stable Afghan government.

Bonn 2001's success was the result of a clear military advantage, a synchronized U.S. interagency position, thorough bilateral preparation, effective multilateral negotiation, limited objectives, and an empowered U.S. negotiating team. Ten years later, the United States lacks the decisive military edge and the international momentum that it had in 2001. However, the United States has a much better understanding of the different Afghan factions and their interests. The Afghan government has structure, is growing in overall effectiveness and anticorruption efforts, and has a vision in the form of empowered subnational governance. The attainment of our initial objective—a stable, broad-based Afghan government that does not provide safe haven to terrorists—requires strong and public U.S. commitment through the rest of this decade. The cost of failure is outlined by Admiral Michael Mullen: "I believe if we walk away from that part of the world, we'll be back in 10 or 20 years. It'll be much more viral than it is right now, as has been the case, since we left in 1989. So I think we all have to work together to keep this going, to bring the pressure we can, and to try—in particular, on the development side, the economic side."[75]

Notes

[1] A loya jirga is a traditional Afghan assembly.

[2] United Nations (UN), "Agreement on Provisional Arrangements in Afghanistan Pending the Reestablishment of Permanent Government Institutions," December 5, 2001, available at <www.un.org/News/dh/latest/afghan/afghan-agree.htm>.

[3] Phillip Kurata, "Envoy to Afghanistan on Bonn Agreement Success," Scoop Independent News, October 7, 2005, available at <http://article.wn.com/view/2005/10/07/Envoy_to_Afghanistan_on_Bonn_Agreement_Success/>. In this State Department press release, Dobbins cites five reasons for Bonn's success: the high level of competence displayed by international civil servants and Afghan leaders, war weariness of the Afghan people, the presence of an internal resistance movement, the active support of Afghanistan's neighbors, and "modest, limited U.S. objectives."

[4] Kenneth Katzman, *Afghanistan: Post-Taliban Governance, Security, and U.S. Policy*, Congressional Research Service (CRS), RL30588 (Washington, DC: CRS, July 25, 2011), 6.

[5] UN, UN Security Council Resolution 1368, September 12, 2001, available at <www.un.org/News/Press/docs/2001/SC7143.doc.htm>.

[6] U.S. Congress, Joint Resolution 23 (Use of Force Resolution), September 14, 2001, available at <www.pbs.org/newshour/updates/terrorism/july-dec01/jr_09-14.html>.

[7] Katzman, *Afghanistan: Post-Taliban Governance, Security, and U.S. Policy*.

[8] Gary Berntsen and Ralph Pezzullo, *Jawbreaker: The Attack on Bin Laden and Al Qaeda: A Personal Account by the CIA's Key Field Commander* (New York: Three Rivers Press, 2005), 168.

[9] James Dobbins, *After the Taliban: Nation Building in Afghanistan* (Washington, DC: Potomac Books, Inc., 2008), 46.

[10] Ibid.

[11] Ibid., 47.

[12] Ambassador Jeffrey Lunstead, telephone interview by authors, May 23, 2011.

[13] Dobbins, *After the Taliban*, 19.

[14] Ibid.

[15] Ibid.

[16] Ambassador James Dobbins, interview by authors, May 26, 2011.

[17] Dobbins, *After the Taliban*, 23.

[18] Dobbins interview.

[19] Dobbins, *After the Taliban*, 30.

[20] Ibid., 31.

[21] Ibid., 32.

[22] Ibid.

[23] Ibid., 36.

[24] Kenneth Katzman, *Afghanistan: Politics, Elections, and Government Performance*, CRS, RS21922 (Washington, DC: CRS, June 1, 2011), 4.

[25] Ibid.

[26] Ambassador Lakhdar Brahimi, interview by authors, June 1, 2011.

[27] Katzman, *Afghanistan: Politics, Elections, and Government Performance*, 4.

[28] Dobbins, *After the Taliban*, 46.

[29] Ibid., 49.

[30] Ibid., 55.

[31] Ibid., 57.

[32] Ibid., 59.

[33] Ibid., 62.

[34] A small group of British soldiers arrived at Bagram Air Force Base in support of the newly opened British embassy. They did not coordinate this arrival in advance and this greatly displeased the Northern Alliance.

[35] Dobbins, *After the Taliban*, 63.

[36] John Burns, "A Nation Challenged: The Bargaining Alliance in Kabul Will Share Power, U.S. Envoy Reports," *The New York Times*, November 20, 2001.

[37] Lunstead interview.

[38] Dobbins, *After the Taliban*, 73.

[39] Ibid.

[40] Ibid., 74.

[41] Lunstead interview.

[42] Ibid.

[43] Dobbins interview.

[44] Dobbins, *After the Taliban*, 83.

[45] Lunstead interview.

[46] Dobbins, *After the Taliban*, 90.

[47] Brahimi interview.

[48] Steven Erlanger, "A Nation Challenged: The Politics; Afghan Talks Stall in Bonn on Comments from Kabul," *The New York Times*, December 1, 2001.

[49] Ibid. The press did not have access to the site because Ambassador Brahimi thought that they would be a distraction. At times, however, Dobbins assisted the process by focusing pressure on a certain issue or Afghan faction during a background interview.

[50] Dobbins, *After the Taliban*, 94.

[51] Ibid., 95.

[52] Ibid., 96.

[53] Colin Powell, "20 November 2001 Remarks at a State Department Working Session on Afghanistan Reconstruction," *Foreign Policy Bulletin* 12 (2002), 232–244.

[54] Pervez Musharraf, *In the Line of Fire* (New York: Simon & Schuster, 2006), 201. Musharraf describes Armitage's conversation with the ISI director general as even more direct: "[I]f you choose the terrorists be prepared to be bombed back into the stone age."

[55] Burns.

[56] Kenneth Katzman, *Afghanistan: Current Issues and U.S. Policy*, CRS, RL30588 (Washington, DC: CRS, August 1, 2003), 19.

[57] James Dobbins, "Ending Afghanistan's Civil War—Statement before the Senate Committee on Foreign Relations," March 8, 2007.

[58] Dobbins interview.

[59] Lunstead interview.

[60] Dobbins interview.

[61] Ibid.

[62] Thomas Johnson, "Afghanistan's Post-Taliban's Transition: The State of State Building after the War," *Central Asian Survey*, March–June 2006, 22.

[63] Lakhdar Brahimi, interview by Mary Sack and Cyrus Samii, *Journal of International Affairs* 58 (Fall 2004), 244. Brahimi believes that the Taliban should have been part of reconciliation measures directly following Bonn.

[64] Mark Sedra, "Consolidating an Elusive Peace: Security Sector Reform in Afghanistan," in *Reform and Reconstruction of the Security Sector*, ed. Alan Bryden and Heiner Hanggi (New Jersey: Transaction Publishers, 2004), 22.

[65] Hillary Clinton, "Remarks at the Launch of the Asia Society's Series of Richard C. Holbrooke Memorial Addresses," New York, February 18, 2011, available at <www.state.gov/secretary/rm/2011/02/156815.htm>.

[66] Katzman, *Afghanistan: Post-Taliban Governance, Security, and U.S. Policy*, 86.

[67] David Cloud, "U.S. to Halve Afghan Forces' Funds," *Los Angeles Times*, September 13, 2011.

[68] Dion Nissenbaum and Maria Abi-Habib, "Afghanistan Halts Taliban Peace Initiative," *The Wall Street Journal*, October 3, 2011.

[69] Brahimi interview, June 1, 2011.

[70] Ibid.

[71] Alissa Rubin, "Clouds Around Karzai Darken the Road Ahead," *The New York Times*, July 13, 2011, available at <www.nytimes.com/2011/07/14/world/asia/14kabul.html?ref=hamidkarzai>.

[72] Islamic Republic of Afghanistan, "Sub-national Governance Policy," Independent Directorate of Local Governance, Spring 2010.

[73] Katzman, *Afghanistan: Politics, Elections, and Government Performance*, 5.

[74] Ashley Tellis, *Reconciling with the Taliban* (Washington, DC: Carnegie Endowment for International Peace, 2009), 35, available at <http://carnegieendowment.org/files/reconciling_with_taliban.pdf>.

[75] Michael Mullen, "U.S. Won't Leave Afghanistan Says Mullen," *The Nation*, June 16, 2011.

About the Authors

Colonel Mark Fields, USA, is an Army Infantry Officer and Senior Military Fellow in the Center for Strategic Research, Institute for National Strategic Studies, at the National Defense University. He holds a Bachelor's degree in Civil Engineering from The Johns Hopkins University and Master's degree in National Security Studies from the National War College.

Ramsha Ahmed is a student at Baylor University and is pursuing a degree in International Studies.